For Anna, my co-conspirator in all things silly.
Thank you for always encouraging my wacky ideas and giving them wings.
—L.B.S.

For Noah, Josh, and Ben
—A.R.

HarperCollins Children's Books, a division of HarperCollins Publishers,
195 Broadway, New York, NY 10007

HarperCollins Publishers, Macken House,
39/40 Mayor Street Upper, Dublin 1, D01 C9W8, Ireland

Clarion Books is an imprint of HarperCollins Publishers.

Do Bees Pee? The Curious and Amazing Ways Nature Avoids Poo-llution

harpercollins.com

Library of Congress Control Number: 2025015529
ISBN 978-0-06-326463-2

The artist used Procreate and Photoshop to create the digital illustrations for this book.

26 27 28 29 30 RTLO 10 9 8 7 6 5 4 3 2 1
First Edition

DO BEES PEE?

The Curious and Amazing Ways Nature Avoids *Poo*-llution

LINDA BOOTH SWEENEY & ARIEL RUTLAND

CLARION BOOKS
An Imprint of HarperCollins*Publishers*

HAVE YOU EVER SEEN...

a toilet for a tiger?

Or a bathroom for a bee?

What does nature do with all that poo and pee?

LET'S SEE.

If you were a bee...

. . . where would you pee?

Actually, bees don't pee, but they make frass that feeds the grass!

If you were a whale swimming in the deep . . .

. . . would your poo end up in one big heap?

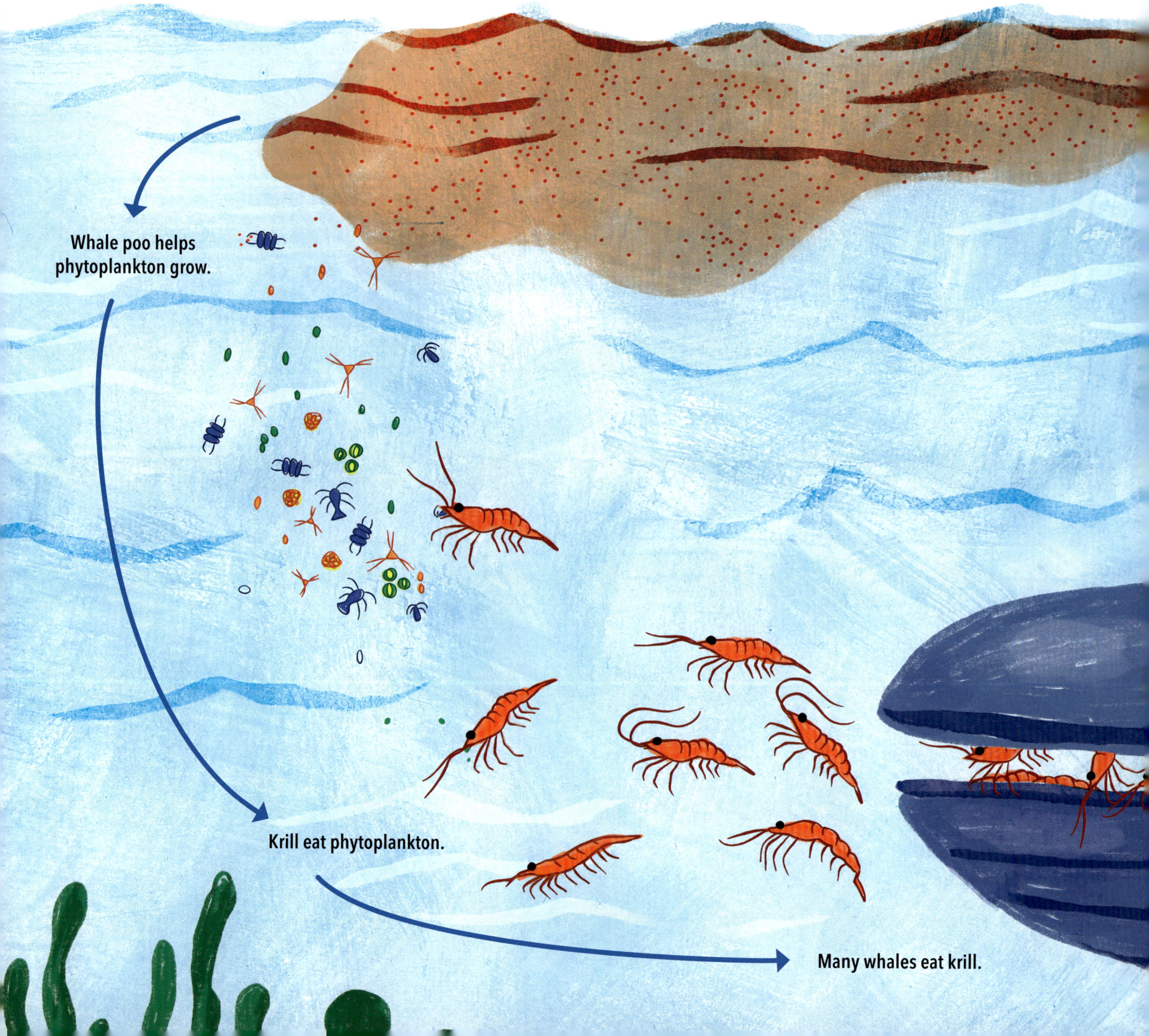

Whale poo, often called a plume, doesn't pile up. It floats to the surface and makes a big, long, colorful, and very smelly cloud in the water. Would you believe the whale poo helps oceans stay healthy and strong?

If you were an elephant wide and tall . . .

. . . would your poo pile up into a ball?

Yes! Some dung beetles roll elephant poo, called dung, into perfect round balls, some as big as apples. They then roll the balls away as fast as they can and eat the dung for lunch. Dung beetles bury elephant poo underground, too, where they lay their eggs in it. Then their young have a tasty treat when they are born!

If you were a parrotfish in the ocean blue . . .

. . . what cool things could you do with poo?

Surprise! Parrotfish poo helps make sand and beaches!

If you were a tiger and made some scat...

. . . what could you possibly do with that?

Tigers use their poo, called scat, to communicate. They mark their territory and tell other tigers, "This is my spot. Go away!" Tiger scat doesn't last long on the ground. Tigers eat other animals, and sometimes bones, fur, and little pieces of meat end up in their scat, making it a tasty snack for other creatures, like beetles and birds.

If you were a bat,

red, black, or brown. . .

. . .would you poo upside down?

Yes! By turning upside down, a bat's droppings, or guano, fall on the ground. Guano feeds many other animals, and plants too!

When you think of poo, you might say, "Ewwww!"

But when it comes to pee and poo,
nature knows just what to do!

Now tap your feet
and feel the beat.
Clap! Clap! Clap!
Let's all sing the Poo Rap!

Feces, Frass,
Plume, Pat,
Turd, Scat,
Pellets, Poo!
(Take a breath!)
Guano, Dung,
Spraints, Goo!
Fewmets, Castings,
Droppings, Doo!

Animal poo on land and sea
keeps nature healthy, strong...
and poo-llution free!

CAN YOU MATCH THE SPECIES WITH ITS FECES?

Castings
Droppings
Dung
Fewmets
Frass
Guano
Pat
Pellets
Plume
Scat
Spraints

(Find the answers at the end of the book.)

Deer
Bird
Bat
Elephant
Tiger
Worm

MORE ABOUT ANIMAL POO AND PEE

BEES

Bee frass contains tiny pieces of poop, leftover food, wax, and other things that bees don't need anymore. Their frass has good stuff that plants need, including nitrogen. When it falls on the ground, it feeds the plants and helps them grow. Many of the plants then make pollen, which the bees come back to eat!

You may have seen bee frass. It can leave sticky yellow streaks on cars, playgrounds, or even windows if bees are flying nearby.

WHALES

Whale poo goes on an amazing journey called the "poop loop," also known as the whale pump. Here's how it works: Whales dive deep to feed. When they come back up, they release poo filled with nitrogen and iron that helps tiny plants called phytoplankton grow. These little plants float in the water. Phytoplankton are then food for other ocean animals, like zooplankton, and smaller fish, like krill and salmon, and for bigger animals, like sharks and whales. So when whales poop, they help the whole ocean stay healthy and full of life.

ELEPHANTS

Elephants eat lots and lots of plants. As they walk and poop, elephants spread different kinds of seeds that are in their dung. These seeds grow into plants that help make food and homes for many animals, like birds, monkeys, and even other elephants! The dung also keeps the soil soft and helps it hold water, making it easier for plants to grow and for savannas, grasslands, and forests to stay healthy. Elephant pee doesn't go to waste either; it is happily slurped up by thirsty birds and insects.

PARROTFISH

Hungry parrotfish eat algae and dead coral off rocks. When they eat, they also crunch up pieces of coral in their tummies. After the coral passes through their digestive tract (or goes through their bodies), it comes out as sand in their poop! Scientists think that 70 percent of the sand on white beaches in places like Hawaii and the Caribbean is actually parrotfish poop. One parrotfish can poop out over a ton of sand a year, which weighs about as much as a car.

TIGERS

Tiger poop might look like a mess, but it's really a treasure! Tiny creatures such as worms, bacteria, and even dung beetles love to munch on it. These creatures, called decomposers, break down the poop and turn it into food for the soil, helping plants grow strong.

When scientists want to know how healthy tigers are, they look at tiger poop! By studying the poop, they can figure out how many tigers live in the area, where they go, and what they eat.

BATS

Bat poop, called guano, is full of good things like nitrogen and phosphorus that help plants grow. When it mixes with dirt, the guano becomes food for special plants like mosses, which create homes for tiny insects and help keep a cave balanced and healthy. When guano falls on a cave floor, bacteria and fungi break it down and make it into yummy food for bugs, including beetles and crickets. Then those bugs become food for bigger animals, like frogs, salamanders, and even bats!

HUMANS

We repurpose cow poo to become fertilizer for the grass the cows eat (a closed loop system); we turn elephant poo into materials such as paper and building blocks; we turn human poo into "poop logs" (after a good amount of processing) that can be burned and used as fuel to cook our food; we also use special bacteria to decompose human poo in biodigesters, which can then be turned into fertilizers to grow food.

MORE TO READ

For kids:

Hevron, Amy. *Poo Pile on the Prairie*. New York. Beach Lane Books, 2025.

Montgomery, Heather L. *Who Gives a Poop? Surprising Science from One End to the Other.* Illustrated by Iris Gottlieb. New York: Bloomsbury Children's Books, 2020.

Sanchez, Anita. *Scat: The Incredible Science of Wildlife Poop*. New York: Holiday House, 2025.

For adults:

Roman, Joe. *Eat, Poop, Die: How Animals Make Our World*. New York: Little Brown Spark, 2023.

A NOTE TO CAREGIVERS

Dear Grown-ups,

Remember when your child first started to talk about poop, whether from people or the fish in the fish tank or a cow on a farm? That moment often brings scrunched-up noses, loud "ewwwws," or fits of laughter—but it can also open the door to something remarkable: understanding how nature creates perfect systems where nothing is wasted.

In our human world, we've grown used to a *take-make-waste* approach. We extract resources, create products, and discard what we no longer need. But step into a forest, meadow, or tide pool, and you'll discover a different story—one where waste simply doesn't exist.

As you read this book with your little one, I invite you to celebrate these magical closed loops together. When a bird's droppings fertilize a seed, when dung beetles roll elephant poop into perfect balls for their babies, when decomposers turn fallen leaves into rich soil—these aren't just funny facts, but glimpses into nature's ingenious design.

After reading, you can extend the learning by exploring your own backyard or neighborhood park. Look for decomposing leaves, watch worms at work, or notice how fallen fruit becomes food for insects. Ask open questions: "I wonder what will happen to this apple core if we leave it here?" "What creatures might find this useful?" These simple questions nurture a child's curiosity about how things link together in nature, helping them "think in systems," a mindset that will serve them well in understanding our complex world.

My hope is that this playful exploration of poop and pee will spark conversations about how we might design our human systems to better mimic nature's brilliant efficiency—where everything has a purpose and nothing is wasted. Have fun imagining with your child what's possible when we close our own loops!

—Linda Booth Sweeney

With gratitude to biologist Joe Roman, author of Eat, Poop, Die *for his many reviews of the manuscript!*

FRASS
BEE

PLUME
WHALE

PELLETS
RABBIT

SPRAINTS
OTTER

FEWMETS
DEER